Mel Bay's

Electric Bass Method – 2

By Roger Filiberto

This book is the second book of this series for the electric bass.

The harmony hints and theory chapters are well-treated for the development of musicianship.

We highly recommend these books to anyone desirous of playing the electric bass as a musician.

A recording of the music in this book is now available. The publisher strongly recommends the use of this recording along with the text to insure accuracy of interpretation and ease in learning.

1 2 3 4 5 6 7 8 9 0

ROGER FILIBERTO

ROGER FILIBERTO NEEDS NO INTRODUCTION TO THE GUITAR WORLD AS HIS STUDENTS ARE SOME OF THE FINEST ARTISTS IN AMERICA TODAY.

HIS BACKGROUND HAS BEEN THAT OF A SUCCESSFUL PROFESSIONAL AND TEACHER. FOR SEVERAL YEARS HE HAS OPERATED ONE OF THE TOP STUDIOS IN THIS COUNTRY LOCATED IN NEW ORLEANS.

HE HAS MADE MANY FINE CONTRIBUTIONS TO THE INSTRUMENT. THIS BOOK ON THE ELECTRIC BASS IS ONE OF HIS FINEST.

IT IS A REAL PLEASURE TO BE ASSOCIATED WITH HIM IN THE PRESENTATION OF THIS TREATISE.

THE TYPES OF INTERVALS

There are FIVE types of intervals.

1. Major
2. Perfect
3. Minor
4. Diminished
5. Augmented

THE MAJOR INTERVALS

The interval will be Major if the upper tone belongs to the key of the lower tone.

The NUMBER NAMES of the Major intervals are 2nd, 3rd, 6th and 7th.

THE PERFECT INTERVALS

The interval will be PERFECT if the upper tone belongs to the key of the lower tone and the lower tone belongs to the key of the upper tone.

The NUMBER NAMES of the Perfect intervals are Primes, 4th, 5th and Octave.

Note that in the example above, the upper note in the Maj. 2nd (d) is in the key of C, the key of the lower tone but the lower note (c) is NOT in the key of the upper tone. (The note c is sharped in the key of D)

The same situation arises in the intervals c-e, c-a and c-b.

The above mentioned intervals will be MAJOR.

In the interval c-f, observe that the upper note (f) is in the key of the lower note (c) and the lower note (c) is in the key of the upper note (f). The same thing occurs in the intervals c-g and c-c.

These intervals will be PERFECT.

INTERVAL MEASUREMENT

UNISONS or PRIMES	0 (no distance)
Major 2nd	1 Step
Major 3rd	2 Steps
Perfect 4th	2½ Steps
Perfect 5th	3½ Steps
Major 6th	4½ Steps
Major 7th	5½ Steps
Perfect Octave	6 Steps

It is advisable to check the distances of the above intervals on a piano or any keyboard instrument.

The distance of each interval should be memorized.

C to D7- to G7-C

This is a Moveable Form

16 Bar Walking Bass Pattern-

In Key of G

Three Chord Cycle

(TONIC- SUB-DOM.- DOM. 7)

I IV7 V7

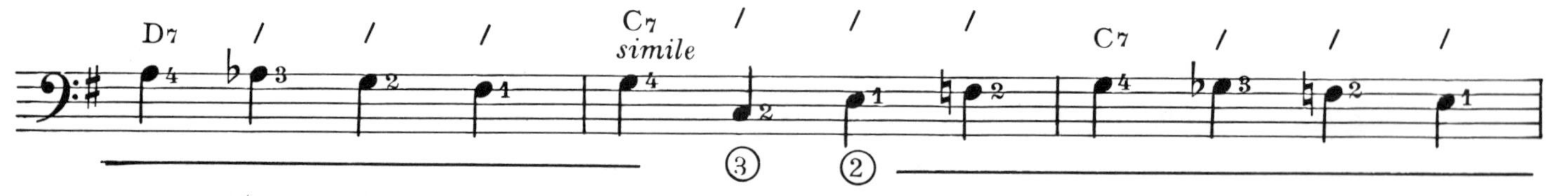

Tonic-Dominant Idea

8 Bar Pattern Key of C

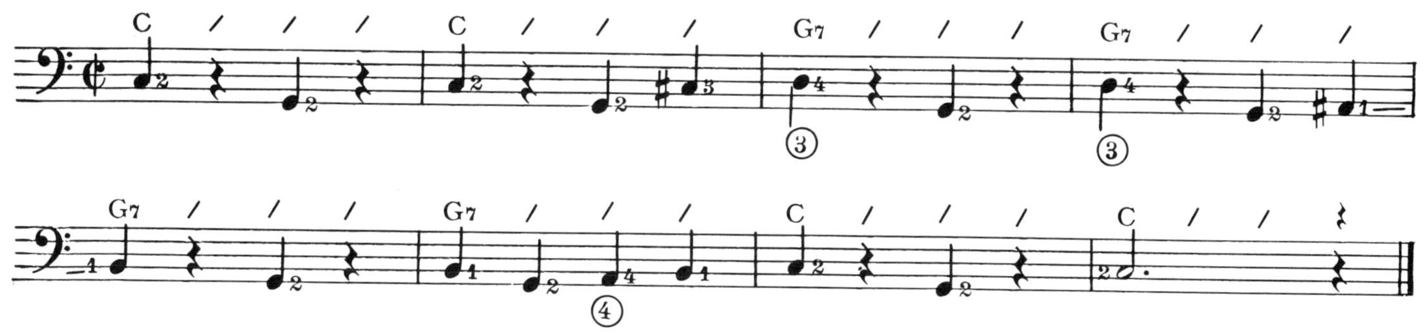

Key of G

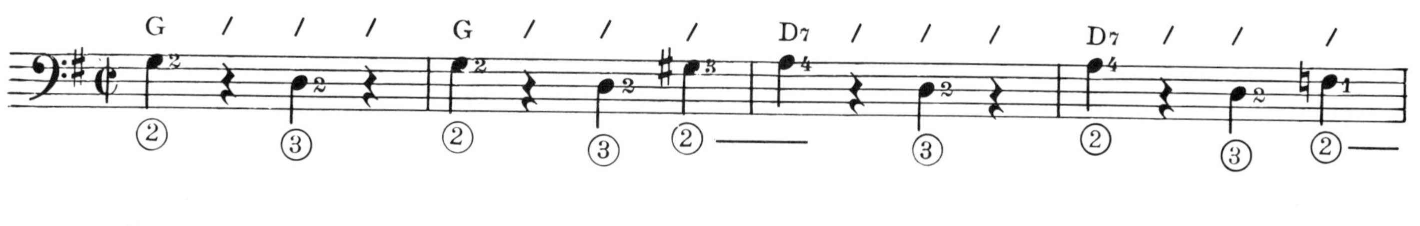

Key of D

Fingering same as Key of C. Two Frets Higher.

Key of A

Fingering same as Key of G. Two Frets Higher.

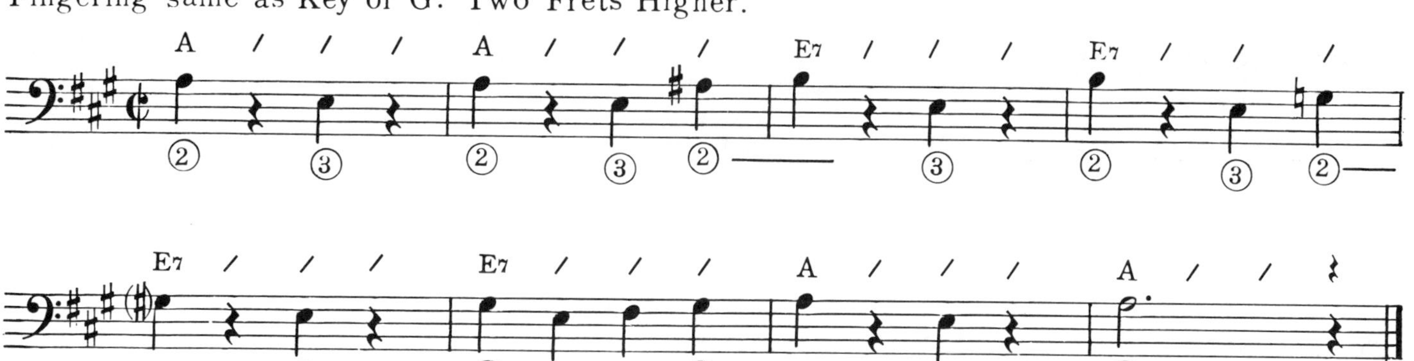

Tonic Dominant Idea

8 Bar Pattern Key of F

Fingering same as Key of G

Key of B♭

Fingering same as Key of G

Key of E♭

Fingering pattern same as Key of C

Key of A♭

Fingering same as Key of G

Major Chords

Triads

The triad is the smallest chord. All chords are based on the triad.

The triad (from tri, meaning three) is built of two thirds placed over each other.

The tones of a triad are the root, (the tone from which the triad is built), the third above, and fifth above.

Triads may be built on each degree of the major and minor scale.

The triads in the major scale are as follows:

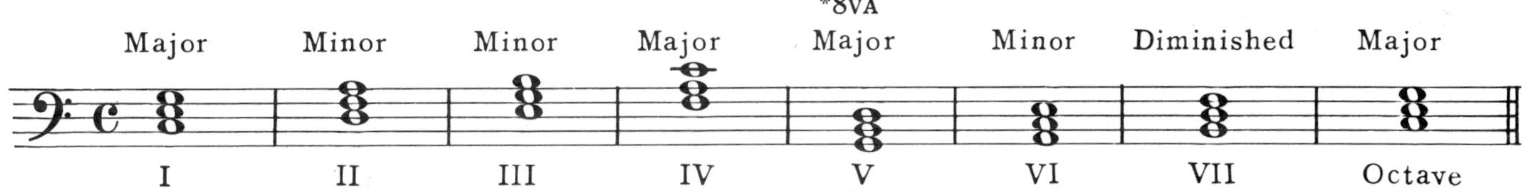

*Play an octave higher. We employ this for easier reading.

The Major Chord

The Major Chord is formed by combining the first, third and fifth tones of the major scale.

The first tone of the scale will be known as the *root* of the chord.

The Major Chord may be arranged in three positions called Inversions.

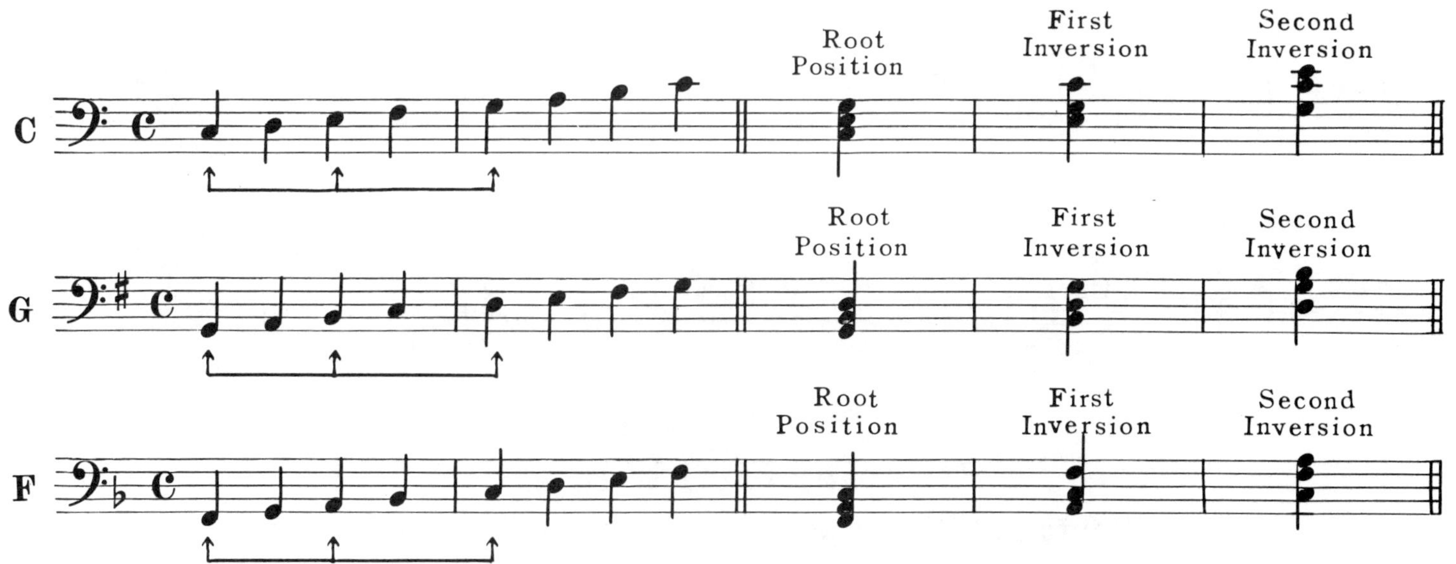

For further study see
Electric Bass Position Studies
by Roger Filiberto

Scale of D Major

In 2nd Position

Study of Third's In D

Using Fingering as in Scale

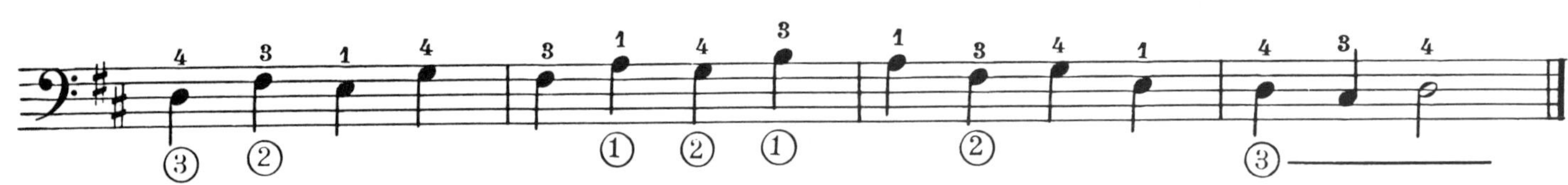

Drink to Me Only With Thine Eyes

Note the use of the G note as the open 1st string and the identical G at the 5th fret of the "D" 2nd string.

Study of Fifth's In D

Pertaining to 3 Princapal Chords in this Key

Walking Bass Pattern In D

Another Walking Bass Pattern In D

For variety and to get the Rock 'n roll or Rhythm and Blues Sound you may substitute the measures illustrated below at the designated measures.

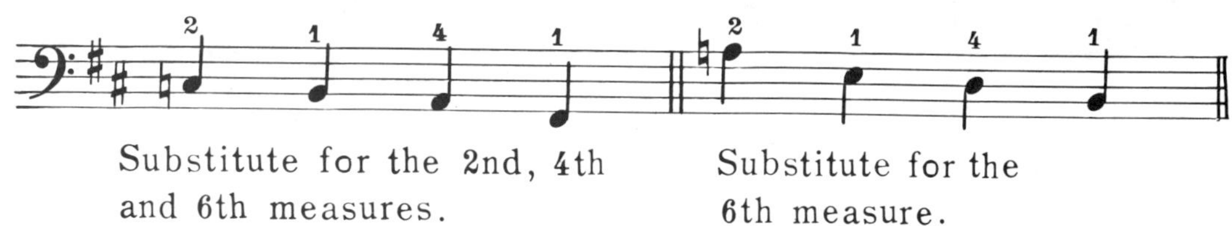

Substitute for the 2nd, 4th and 6th measures.

Substitute for the 6th measure.

Diatonic Study In D

This is a Moveable Pattern

12 Bar Blues Key of D

Pattern Fingering throughout as in first measure

The Minor Chords

The major and minor chords will have the same note-spelling but the third of the minor chord will be ½ step lower. Example: C – c-e-g. Cm – c-e♭-g.

The intervals of the minor chord will be; Root, Mi. 3rd, Perfect 5th.

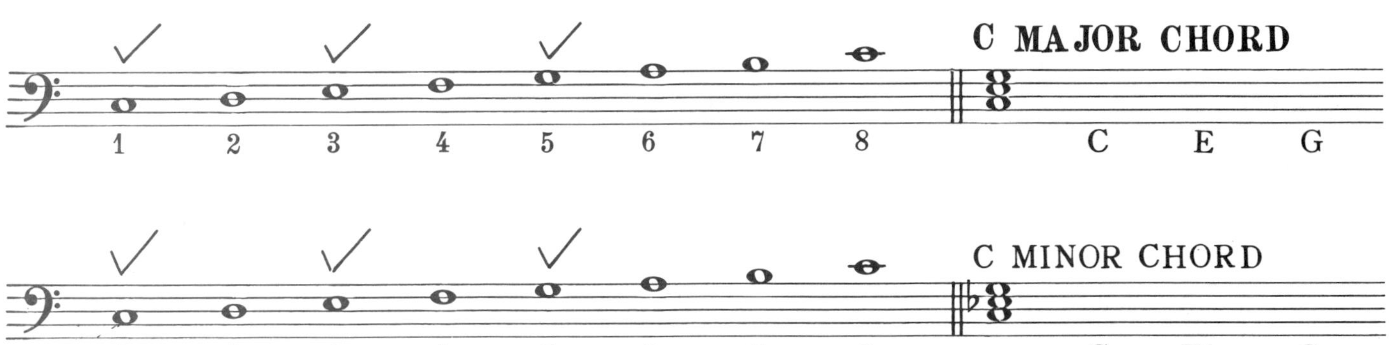

The Notation of the Major and Minor Chords

Memorize but do not play.

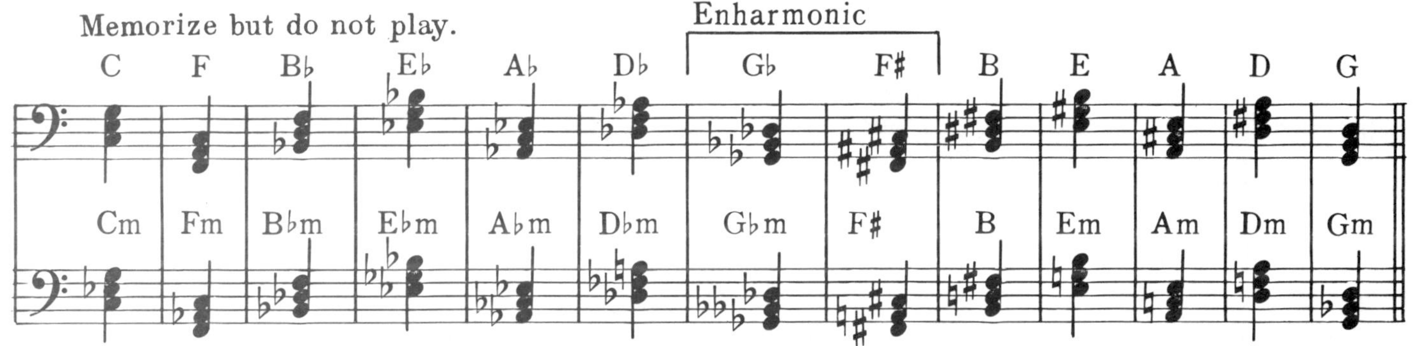

A Table of Major Key Signatures

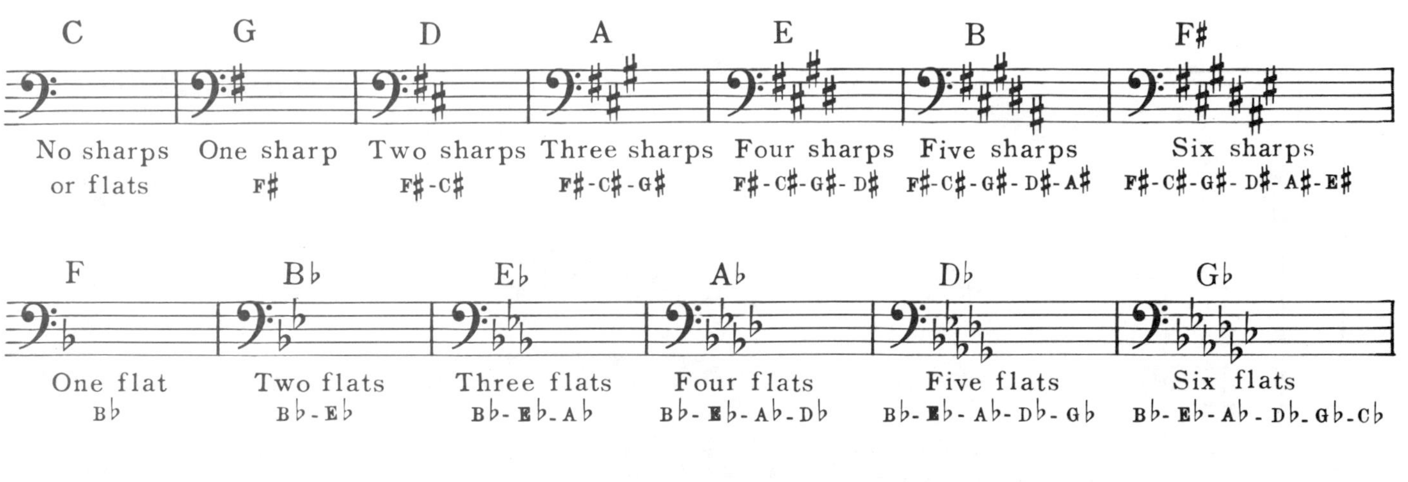

The Major and Relative Minor Keys

C	F	B♭	E♭	A♭	D♭	G♭	F♯	B	E	A	D	G
Am	Dm	Gm	Cm	Fm	B♭m	E♭m	D♯m	G♯m	C♯m	F♯m	Bm	Em

TO BE MEMORIZED

Table of Scales Beginning with 2nd Finger (Moveable Form) same fingering for all Scales.

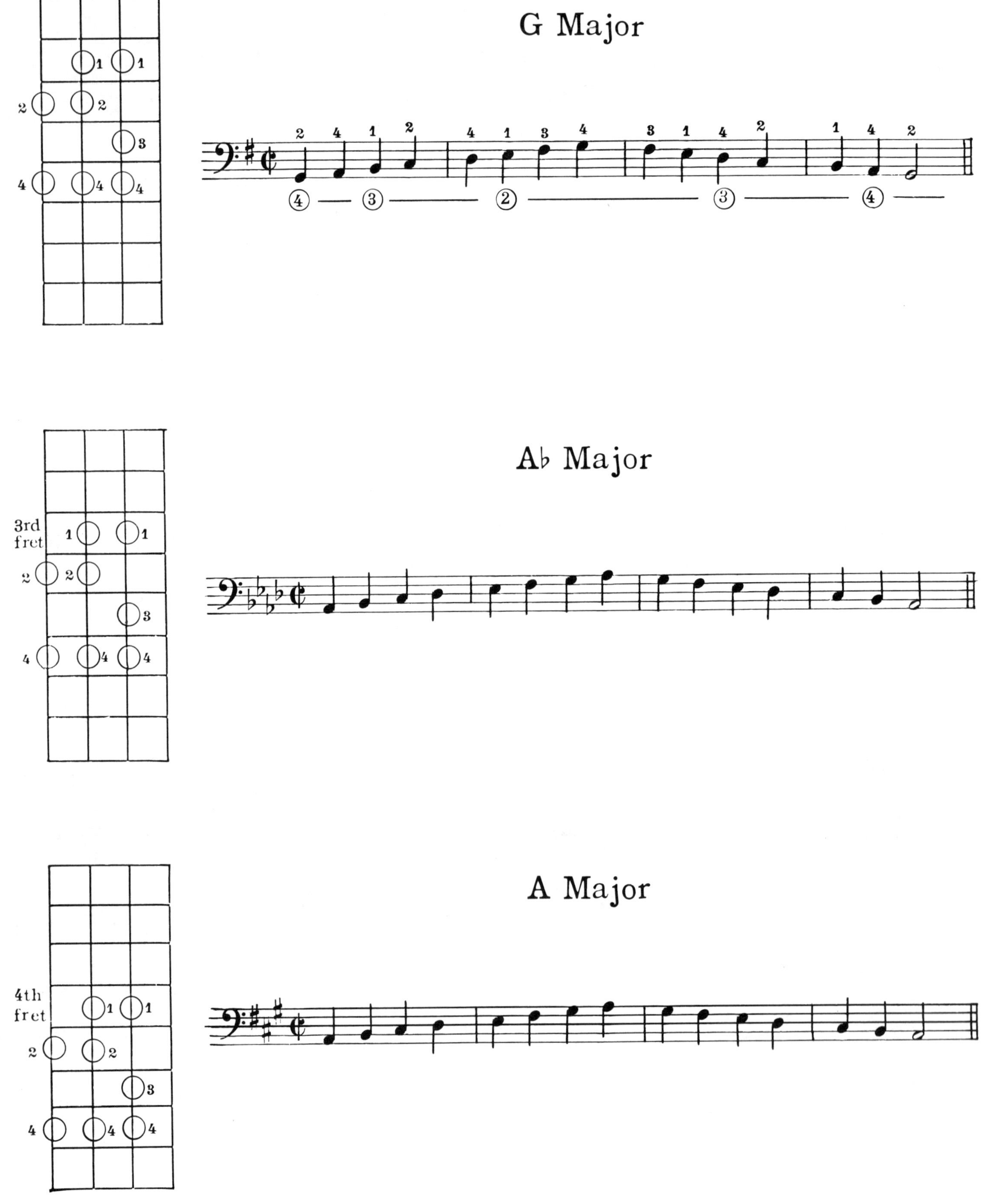

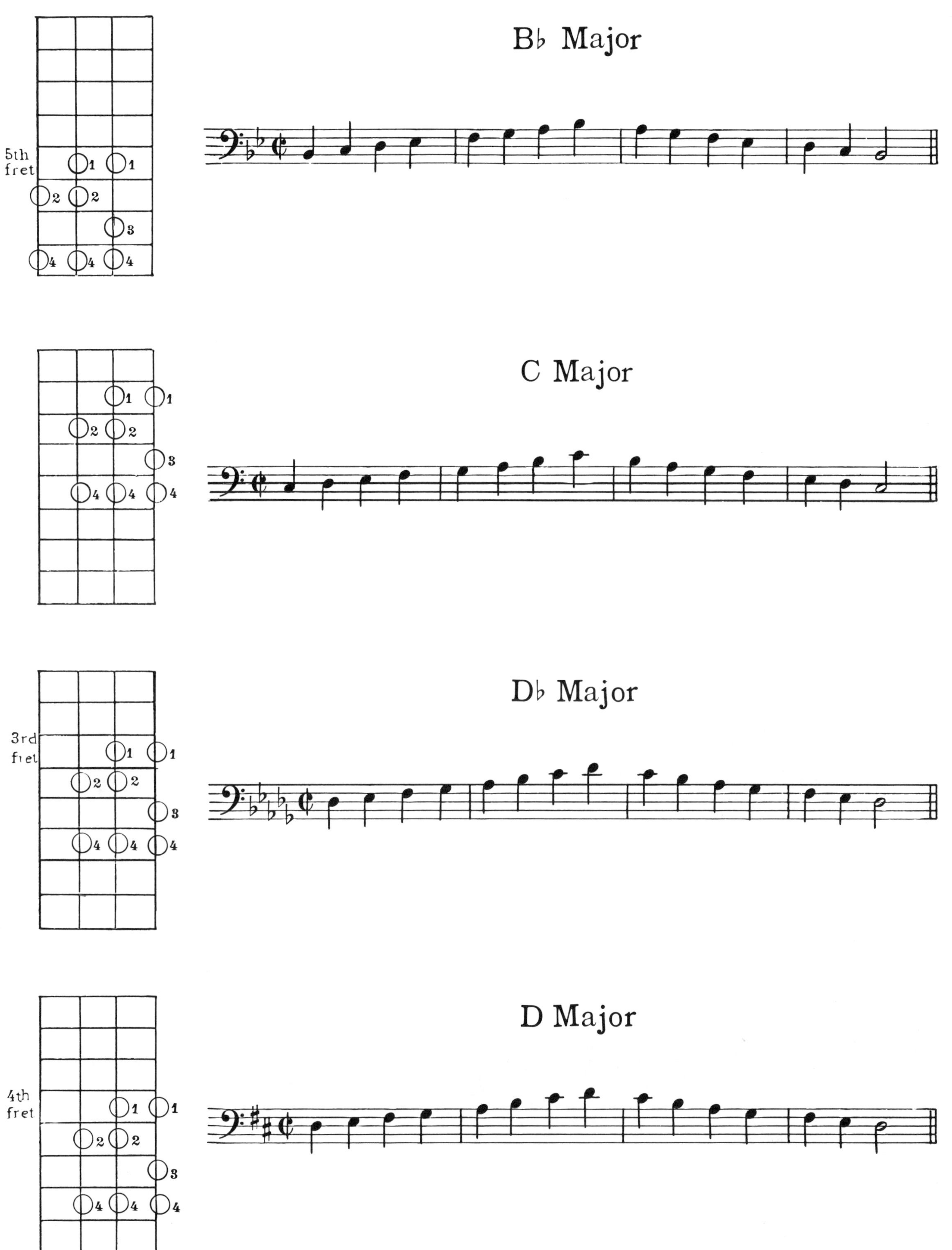
B♭ Major
5th fret
1
1
2
2
3
4
4
4
C Major
1
1
2
2
3
4
4
4
D♭ Major
3rd fret
1
1
2
2
3
4
4
4
D Major
4th fret
1
1
2
2
3
4
4
4

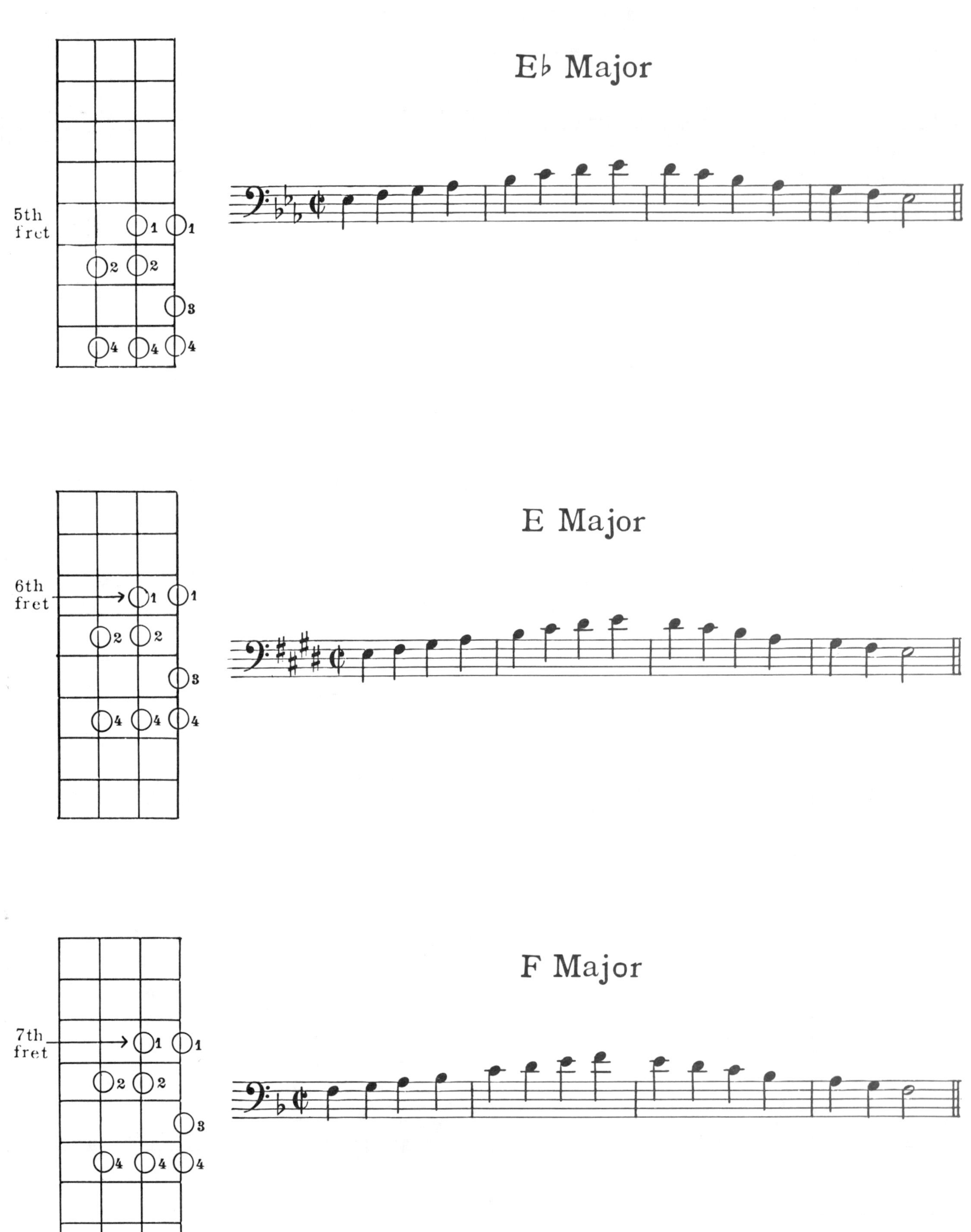
Eb Major
5th fret
1
1
2
2
3
4
4
4
E Major
6th fret
1
1
2
2
3
4
4
4
F Major
7th fret
1
1
2
2
3
4
4
4

The Dominant Seventh Chord

The intervals of the Dominant Seventh Chord are Root, Major 3rd, Perfect 5th and Minor 7th.

The Dominant Seventh in the fundamental or root position will consist of a Ma. 3rd, Mi. 3rd and a Mi. 3rd. (See Constuction)

The Dominant Seventh Chord is named after the dominant (V) degree of the scale. The three principal chords in any major or minor key are the Tonic, Sub-Dominant and Dominant Seventh chords.

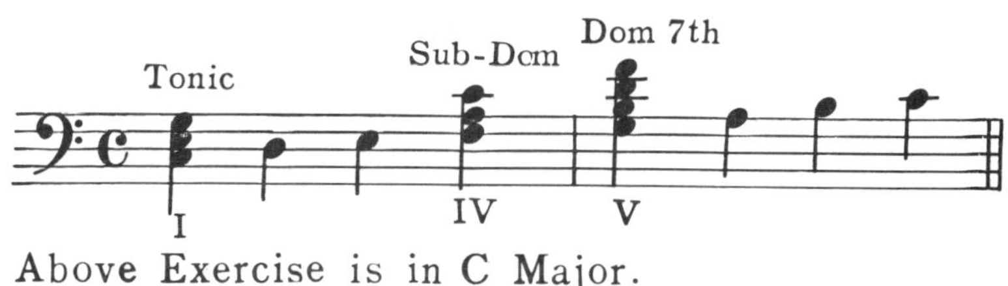

Above Exercise is in C Major.

Construction

The construction of a Dominant Seventh Chord is best accomplished by taking the 1st, 3rd, 5th and *lowered 7th* of any *major scale*.

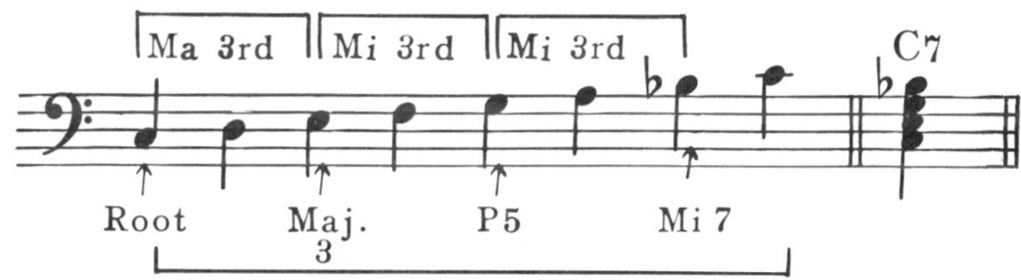

The student must write out all major scales, construct the dominant seventh chords by the above method and memorize the note-spelling of the chords.

The Notation of the Dominant Seventh Chord

8 Bar- 3 Chord Cycle In C

Moveable Pattern
Walking Bass

Cycle No. 1

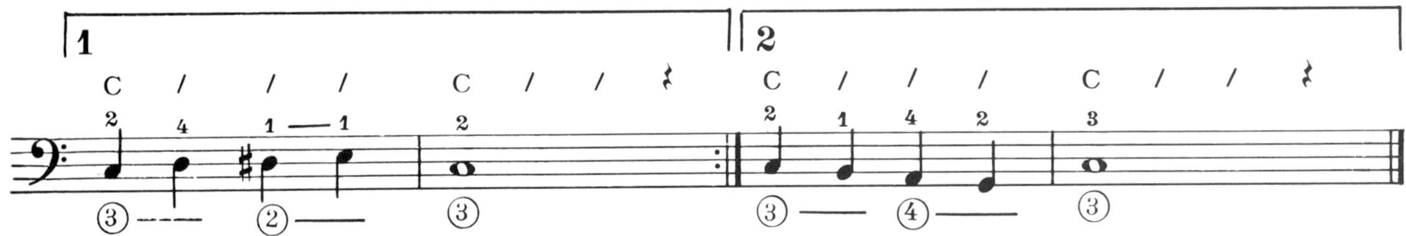

8 Bar- 3 Chord Cycle In D♭

Fingering same as Key of C

Cycle No. 2

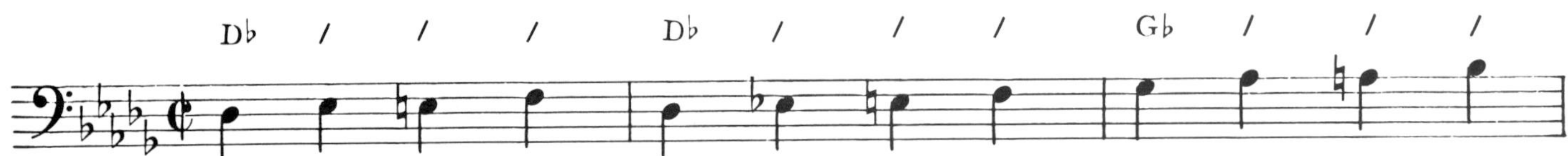

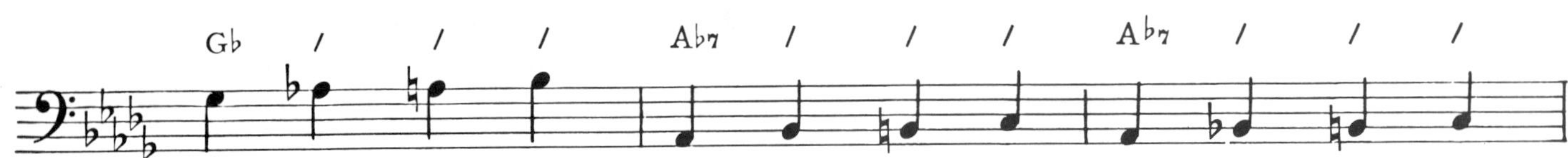

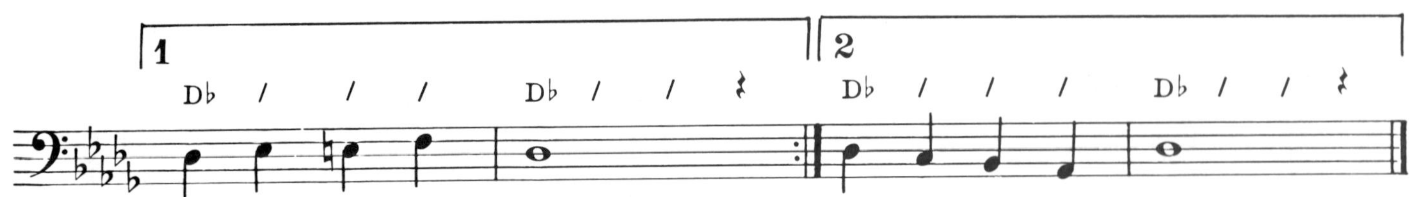

D Major

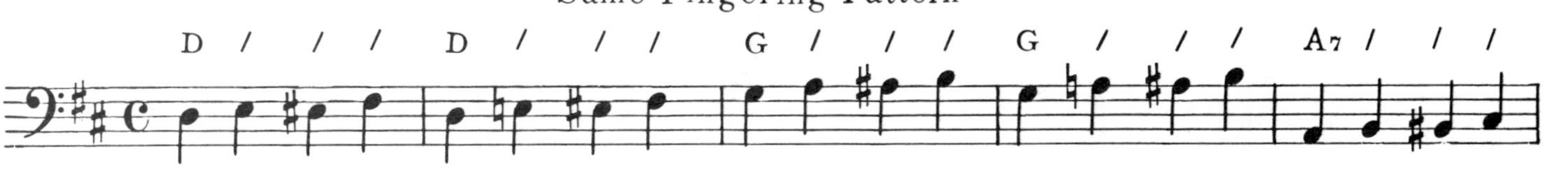

E♭ Major

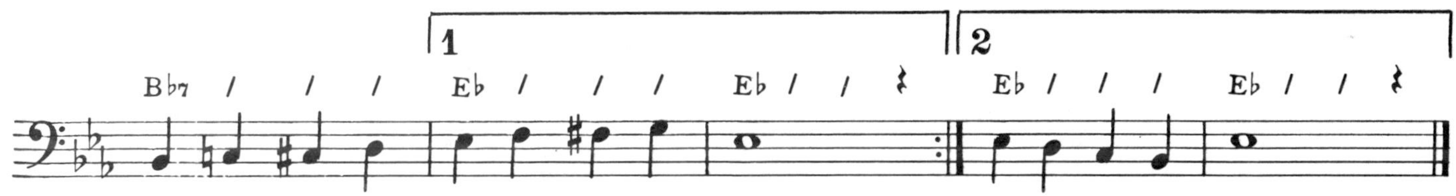

E Major

F Major

Key of G

G / / / G / / / C / / / C / / / D7 / / /

D7 / / / 1 G / / / G / / / 2 G / / / G / /

Key of A♭

A♭ / / / A♭ / / / D♭ / / / D♭ / / / E♭ / / /

E♭ / / / 1 A♭ / / / A♭ / / / 2 A♭ / / / A♭ / /

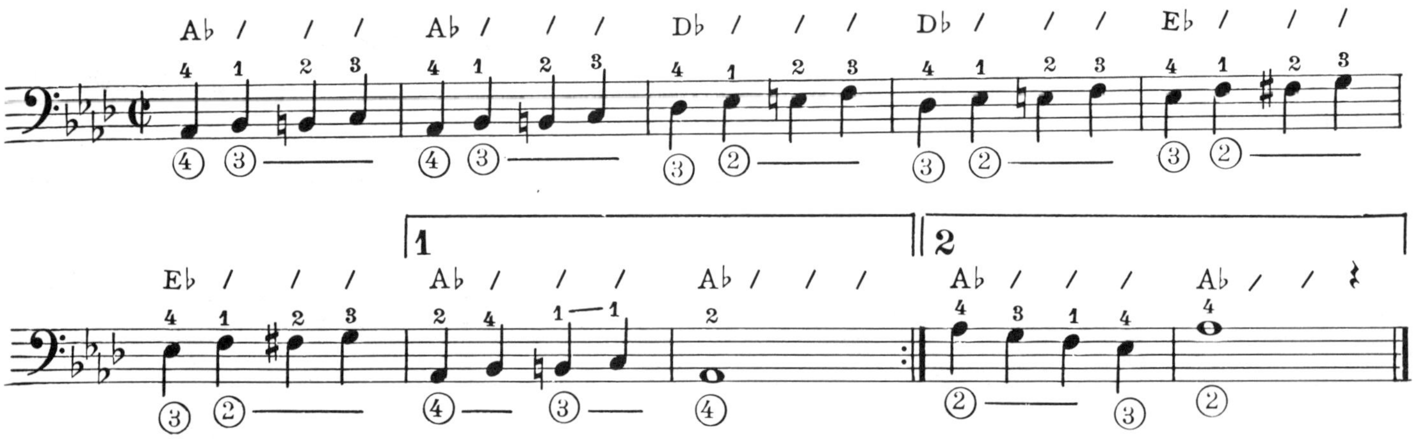

Key of A

Key of B♭

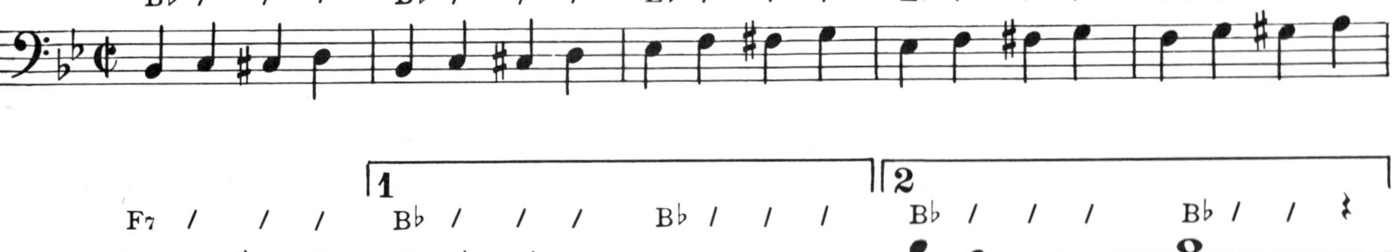

THE AUGMENTED CHORD

The Augmented Chord contains three notes....each a major third apart.

The formula for the Augmented Chord construction is:

Intervals:	Ma 3rd + Ma 3rd	
Steps:	(2)	(2)

The technical terms for the intervals of the Augmented Chord are:

ROOT--MAJOR THIRD--AUGMENTED FIFTH

The symbols for the Augmented Chord are (+) or (aug.). The (+) is the most widely used.

Augmented Chords may be formed on all twelve steps of the Chromatic Scale with each note being the root.

There are only four Augmented Chords. The four chords contain all twelve tones of the Chromatic Scale.

THE NOTE -SPELLING OF THE AUGMENTED CHORD

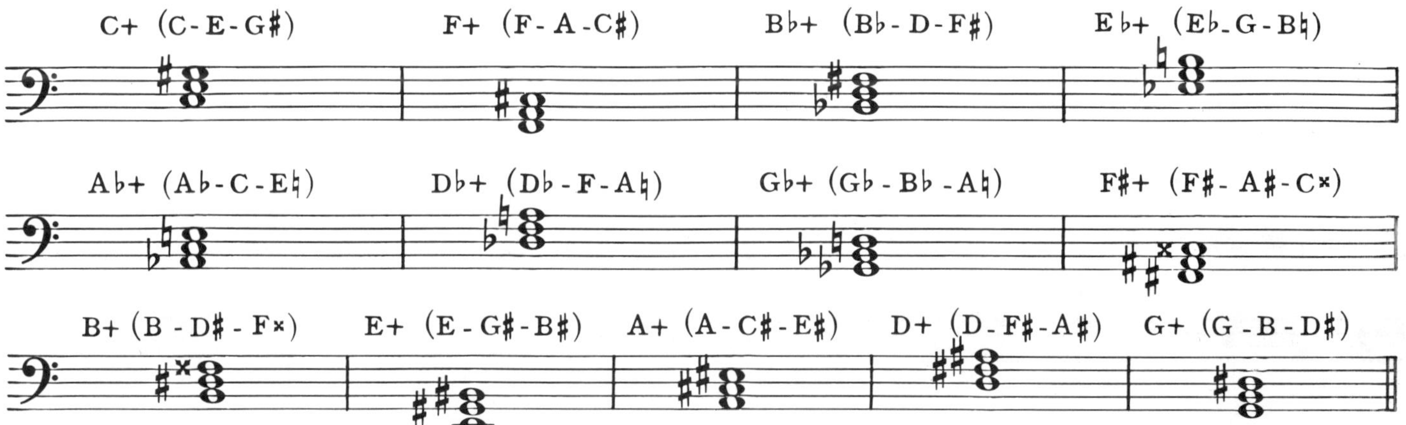

THE HARMONIZED HARMONIC MINOR SCALE

The third chord in the harmonized harmonic minor scale below will be an augmented chord.

The pattern for the construction of triads on each note of the Harmonic Minor scale is:

Mi-Dim-Aug-Mi-Ma-Ma-Dim-Mi
1 2 3 4 5 6 7 8

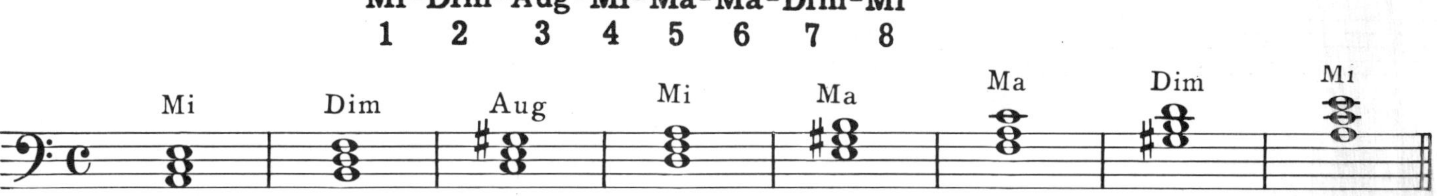

Keep Moving No. 1

WALKING PATTERN IN C

A Study of "CONNECTING LINKS" in Cycle of Fourths.

Keep Moving No. 2

WALKING PATTERN– Same Chord changes as No. 1
Using different approach–

Use of open string is optional. We recommend closed pattern, but do not rule out use of open strings.

THE DIMINISHED SEVENTH CHORD

The Diminished Seventh Chord ranks next in importance to the Dominant Seventh Chord.

The Diminished Seventh Chord contains four notes....each a Minor Third apart. (1½ steps in distance)

The formula for the Diminished Seventh Chord construction is:

Intervals:	Mi3 + Mi3 + Mi3
Steps:	1½ + 1½ + 1½

The technical terms for the intervals of the Diminished Seventh Chord are:

ROOT--MINOR THIRD--DIMINISHED FIFTH--DIMINISHED SEVENTH

The Diminished Seventh Chord may be formed by lowering the 3rd, 5th, and 7th of the Dominant Seventh Chord ½-step or by raising the Root of any Dominant Seventh Chord ½-step.

EXAMPLE

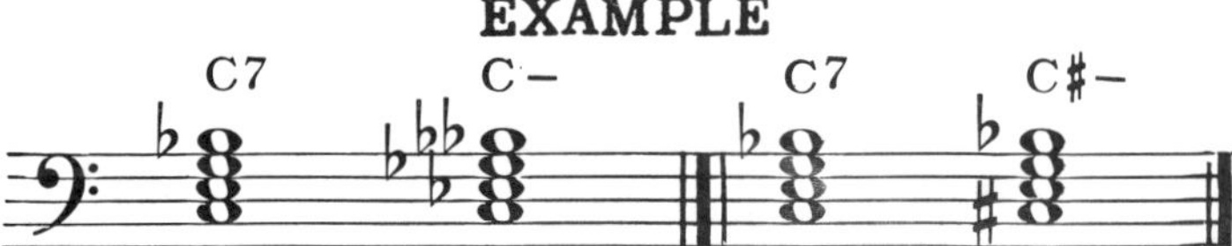

To avoid an excessive amount of double-sharps and double-flats that would occur if we kept the chord spelling correct, we substitute the enharmonic tone as shown in the example below.

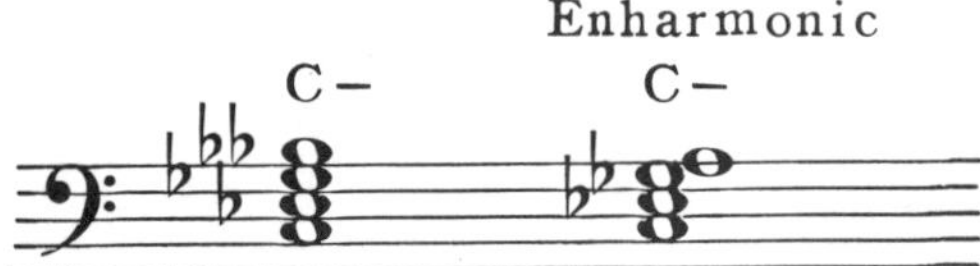

The following note combinations will facilitate chord reading if memorized by the student: F♯ and E♭. C♯ and B♭. G♯ and F♮.

The Diminished Seventh Chord is commonly referred to as the DIMINISHED Chord and will be called that in this course.

The Symbol for the Diminished Chord is (-). Sometimes the abbreviation (dim) is used. The minus sign (-) is preferable and will be used.

Diminished Chords may be formed on all twelve steps of the Chromatic Scale. Each note may be the root.

There are only three diminished chords. The three chords contain all twelve tones of the Chromatic Scale.

THE DIMINISHED CHORDS ON THE CHROMATIC SCALE

All similar chords regardless of enharmonics will be numbered in groups.

The first group will be number I, the second group number II and the third will be III. Note that the tones are the same in each group even though the notation is different.

B♭ Major Scale

BEGINNING WITH 4th FINGER

Walking Bass 3 Chord Pattern in B♭

Fingering pattern same throughout

Practice with open strings in first position, then as indicated.

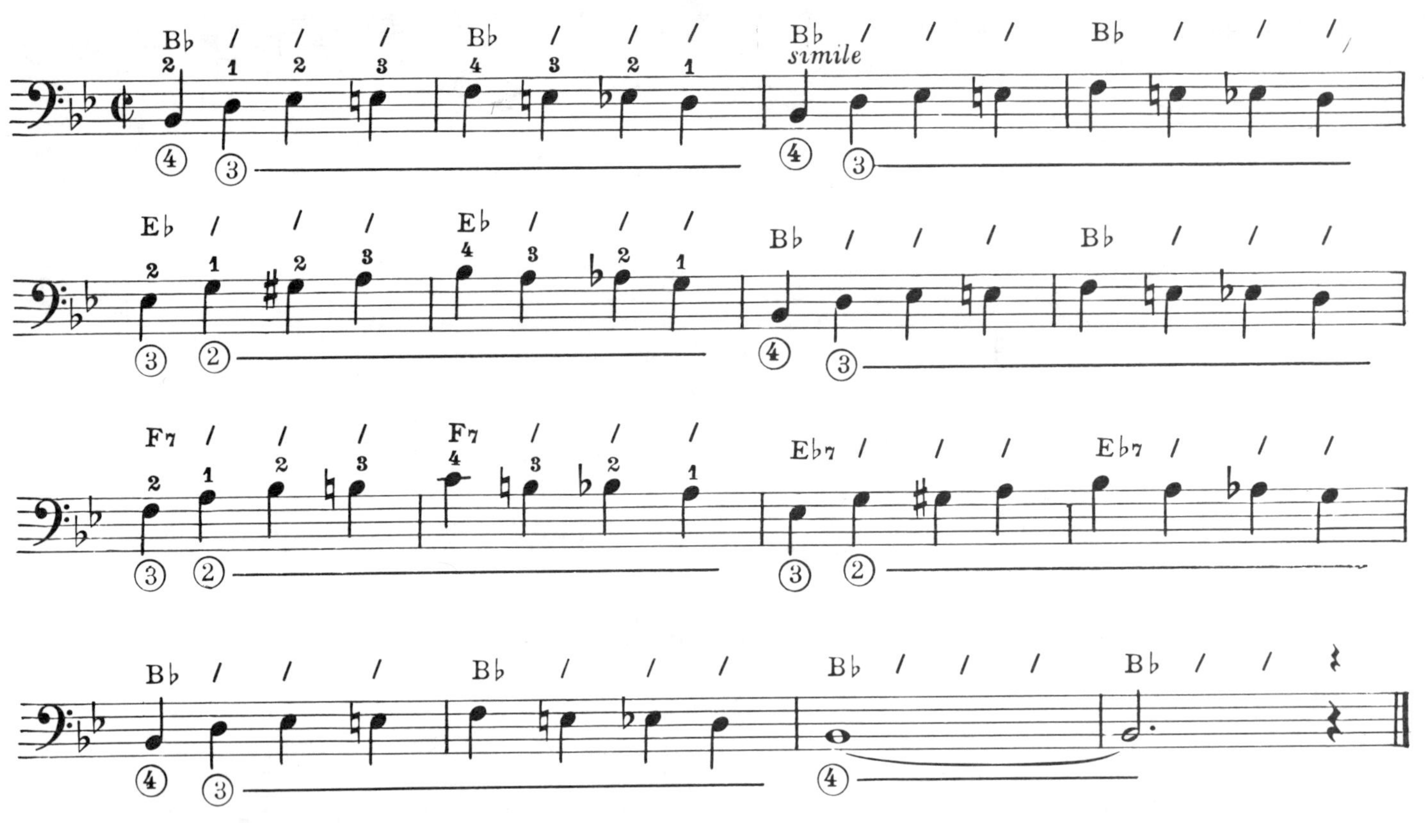

TYPICAL BASS ACCOMPANINET TO THE FOLLOWING CHORD CYCLE in B♭

B♭, G7, C7, F7, B♭ (First Position and 2nd)

For variety substitute C minor for C7. Bass remains the same.

SAME CHORD PATTERN IN "WALKING BASS" STYLE

First Position only

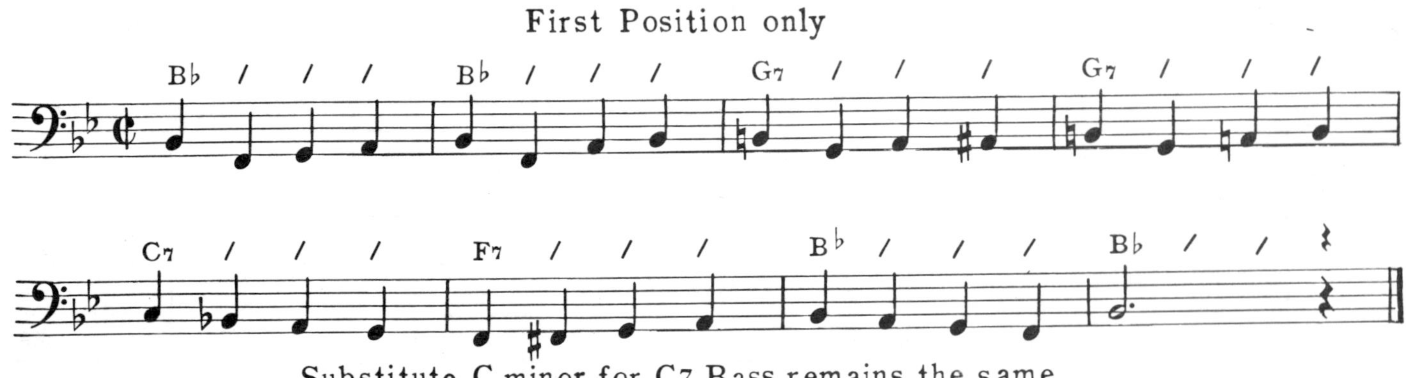

Substitute C minor for C7. Bass remains the same.

Typical Bass Part to the following Chord Cycle In D Major.

D, B7, E7, A7, D – You may substitute EM for E7 without changing bass.

Practice with Open Strings – then as marked.

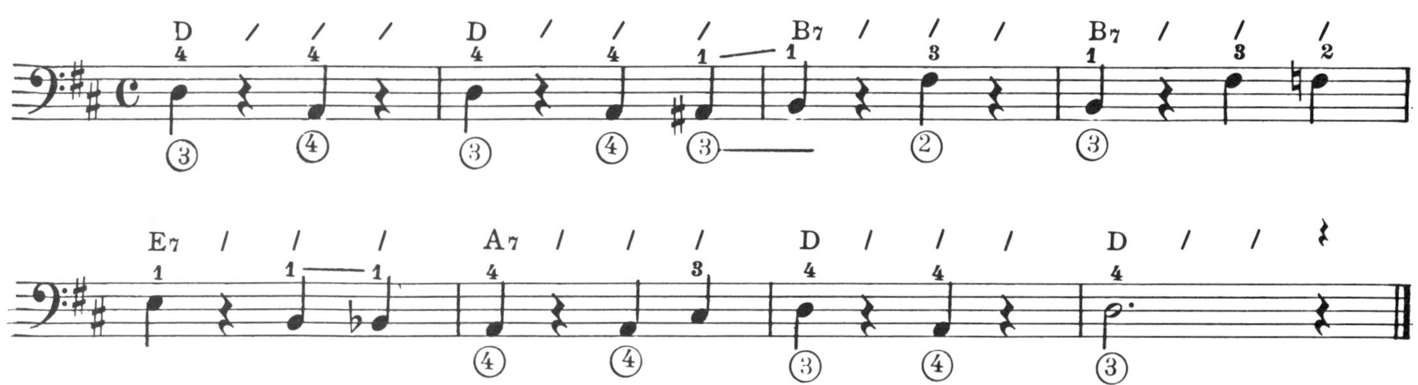

Triplet Study In D

"Walking" Bass Style

First Position using Open Strings

Practice substituting EM for E7– Bass remains unchanged.

V Position Study

12 Bar Rhythm and Blues Study - In Key of C

(Moveable Pattern)

TONIC - SUB-DOM. DOM. 7

TYPICAL BASS PART TO THE FOLLOWING CHORD CYCLE IN C MAJOR

C, A7, D7, G7, C

You may substitute DM for D7 without changing bass part.

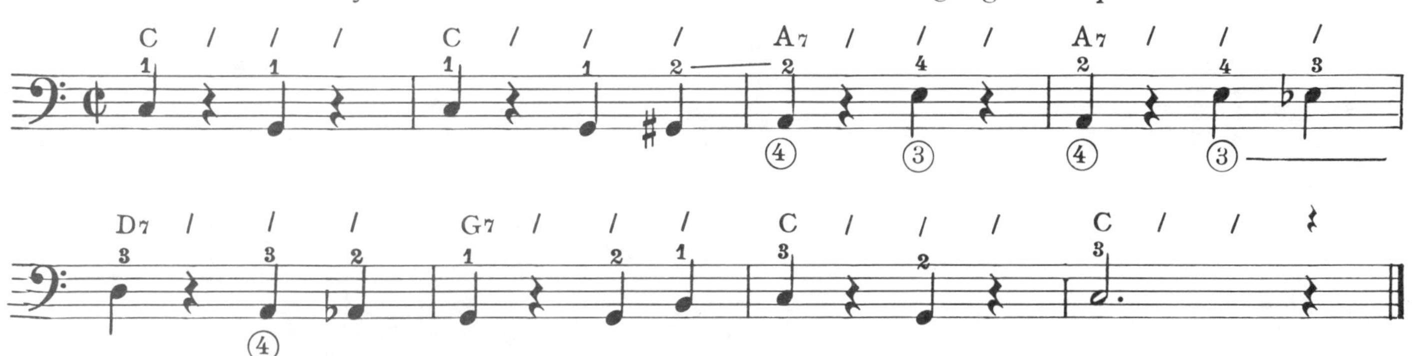

SAME CHORD PATTERN IN "WALKING" BASS STYLE

First Position using Open Strings

Practice substituting DM for D7 – Bass remains unchanged.

Spooky Stuff

A MINOR JAZZ MODE

All in First Position using open strings.

8 Bar 3 Chord Cycle

(1st Position) **Walking Bass Pattern in A minor**

Four Bar Vamp or Intro.

More 4 Bar Intro.

Relaxing

2nd and 4th position (Moveable)

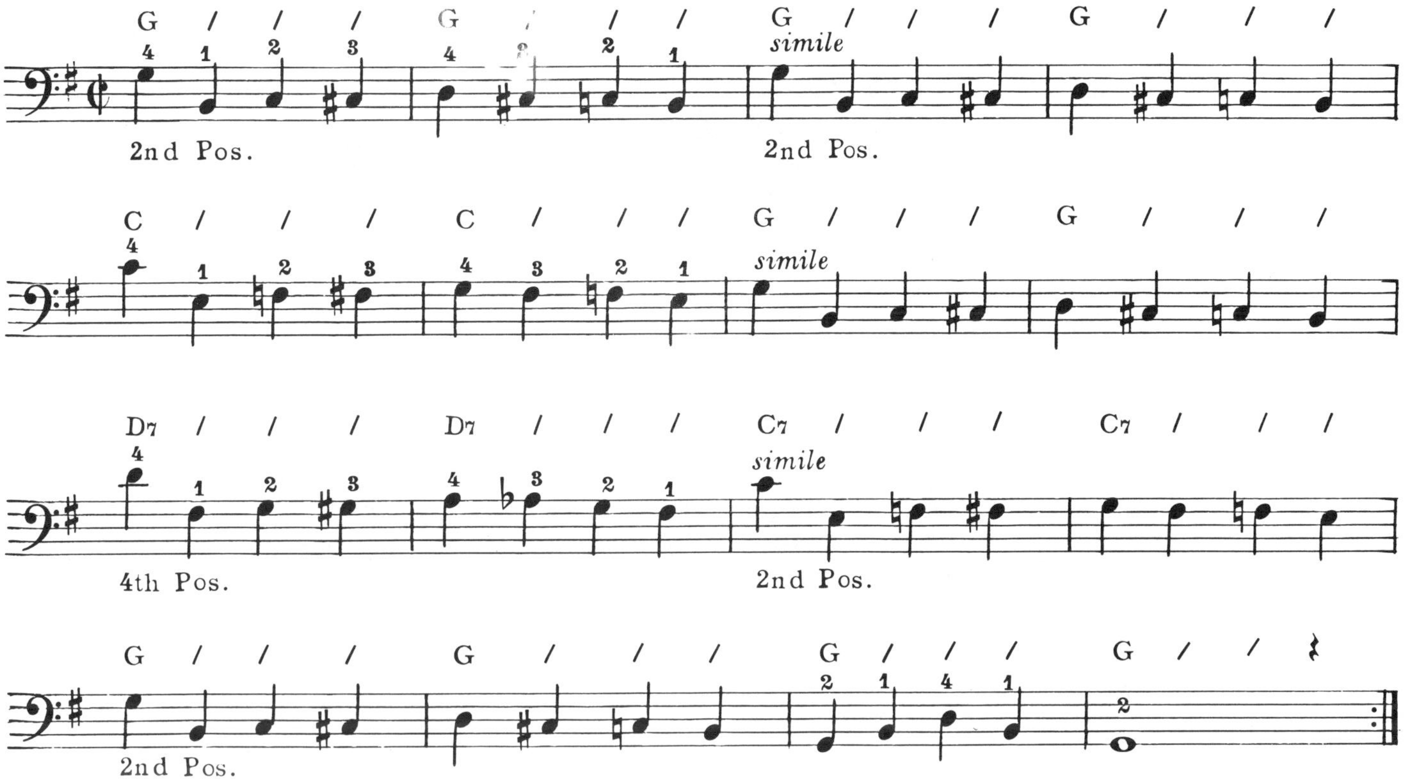
G / / / G / / / G / / / G / / /
simile
2nd Pos.
2nd Pos.
C / / / C / / / G / / / G / / /
simile
D7 / / / D7 / / / C7 / / / C7 / / /
simile
4th Pos.
2nd Pos.
G / / / G / / / G / / / G / /
2nd Pos.

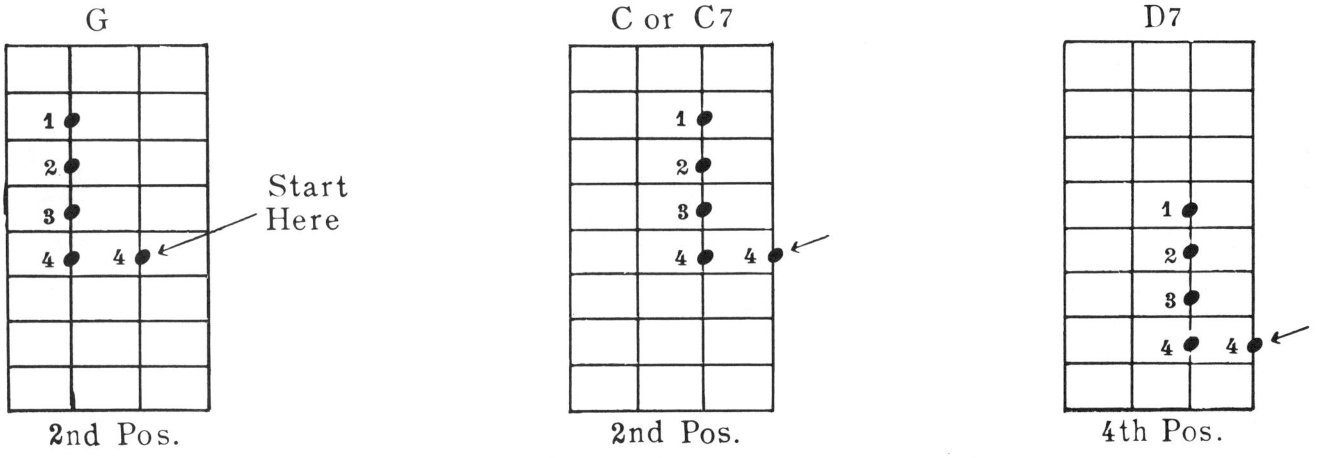
G
Start Here
2nd Pos.
C or C7
2nd Pos.
D7
4th Pos.

Easy Does It

2nd and 4th position (Moveable form)

simile
4th Pos.
2nd Pos.

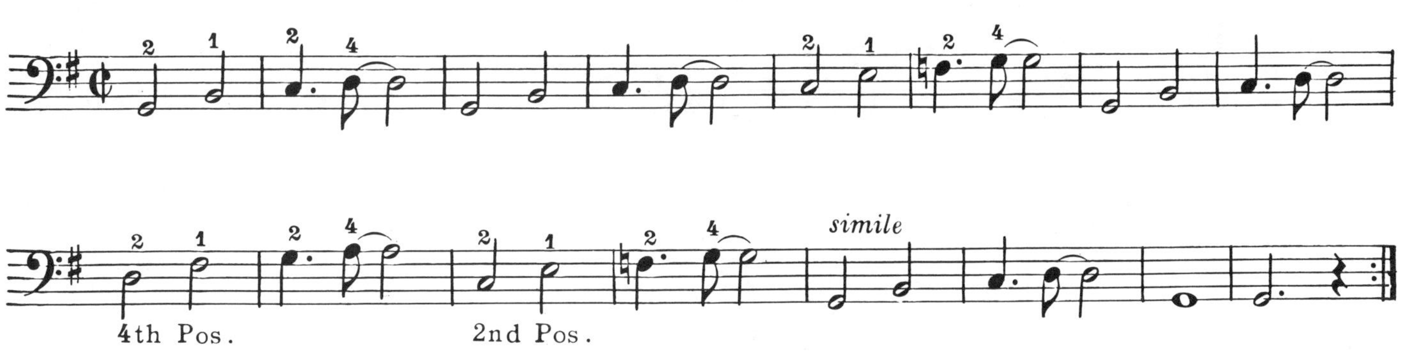

Key Largo Blues - 3 Chord Pattern

2nd and 4th position (Moveable)

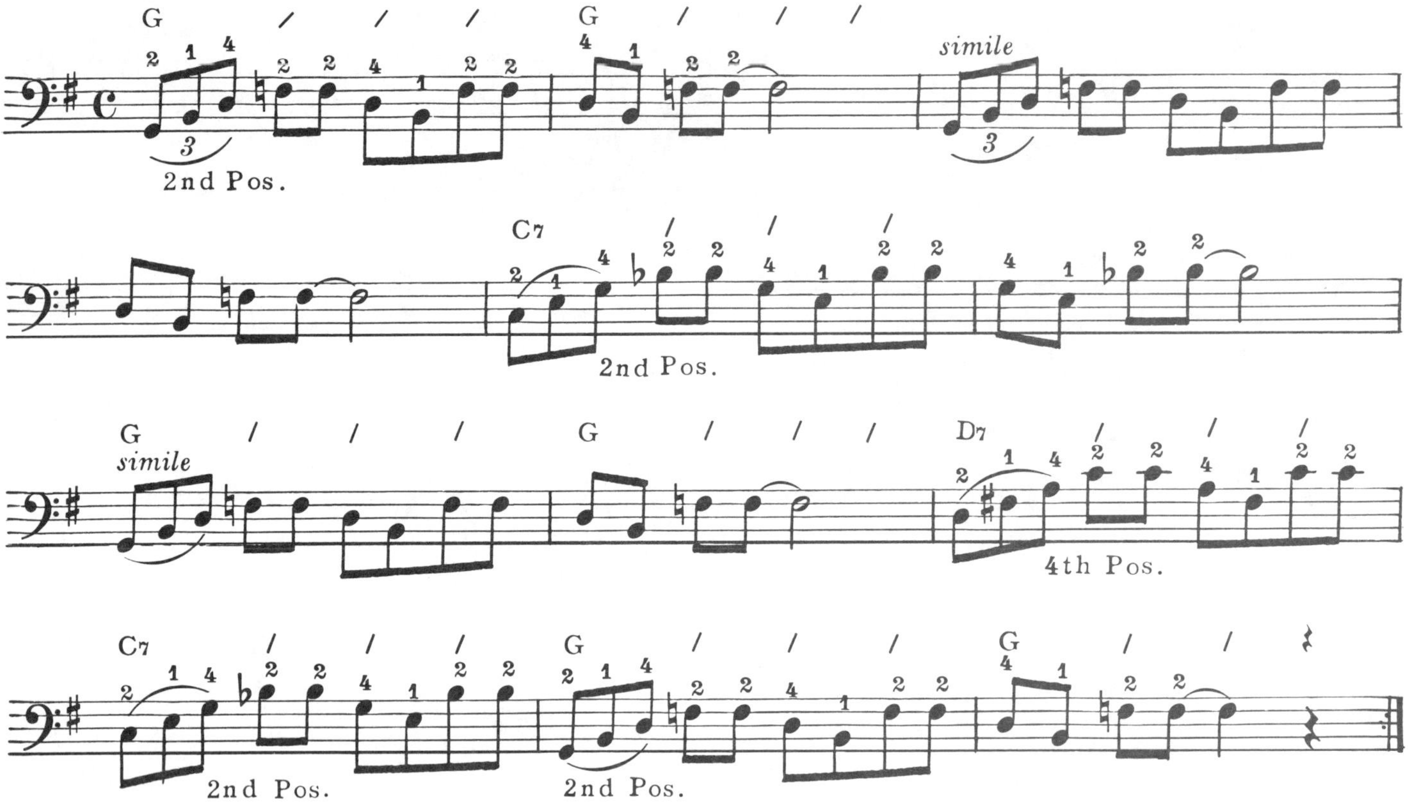

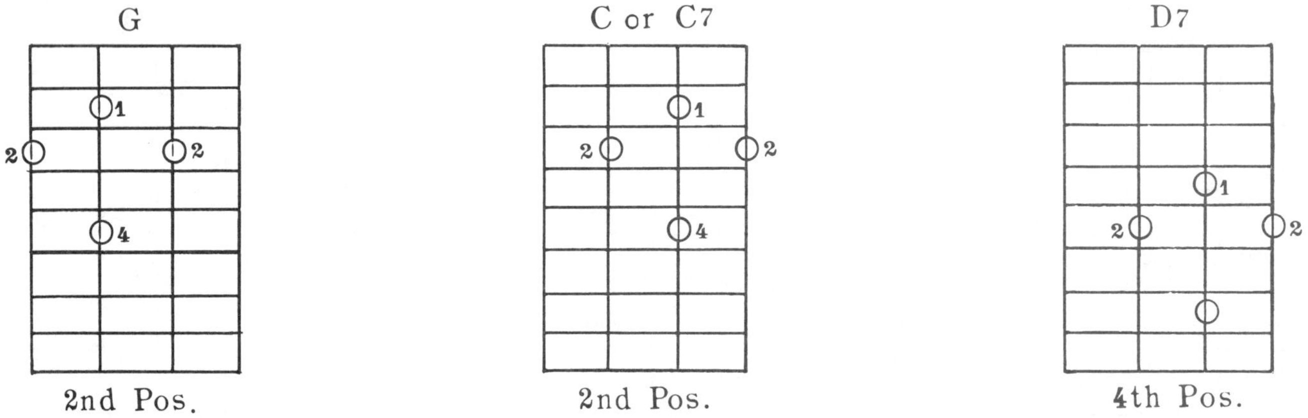

G / / / G / / /
simile
2nd Pos.

C7 / / /
2nd Pos.

G / / / G / / / D7 / / /
simile
4th Pos.

C7 / / / G / / / G / / 𝄽
2nd Pos. 2nd Pos.

G	C or C7	D7
2nd Pos.	2nd Pos.	4th Pos.

(See Book One ARPEGGIO CHART. Page 40)

A Study in Octaves

Typical Bass Part in F with wide Range of Chords

Rhythm and Blues Pattern in G

This is a Moveable Pattern

Study of Thirds in G

More Walking Bass 3 Chord Pattern

KEY OF C

NOTE: You will observe that the C pattern (first four measures) is marked to begin on the fourth string (at 8th fret). This C pattern can also be played starting on the 3rd string (3rd fret) but because the next chord pattern F (5th measure) has to be played at the 8th fret on the third string it is more logical to play the C pattern starting on the 4th string on the 8th fret.

Diatonic Study in Eighth Notes

Rhythm and Blues Pattern in C

This is a Moveable Pattern

NOTE: C pattern beginning on 4th string at the 8th fret is fully explained in previous lesson entitled "More walking Bass three chord pattern key of C".

Rhythm and Blues in E

Walking Bass 3 Chord Pattern

KEY OF G

This is a Moveable Pattern

Diatonic Sequence in G

Tenths Study

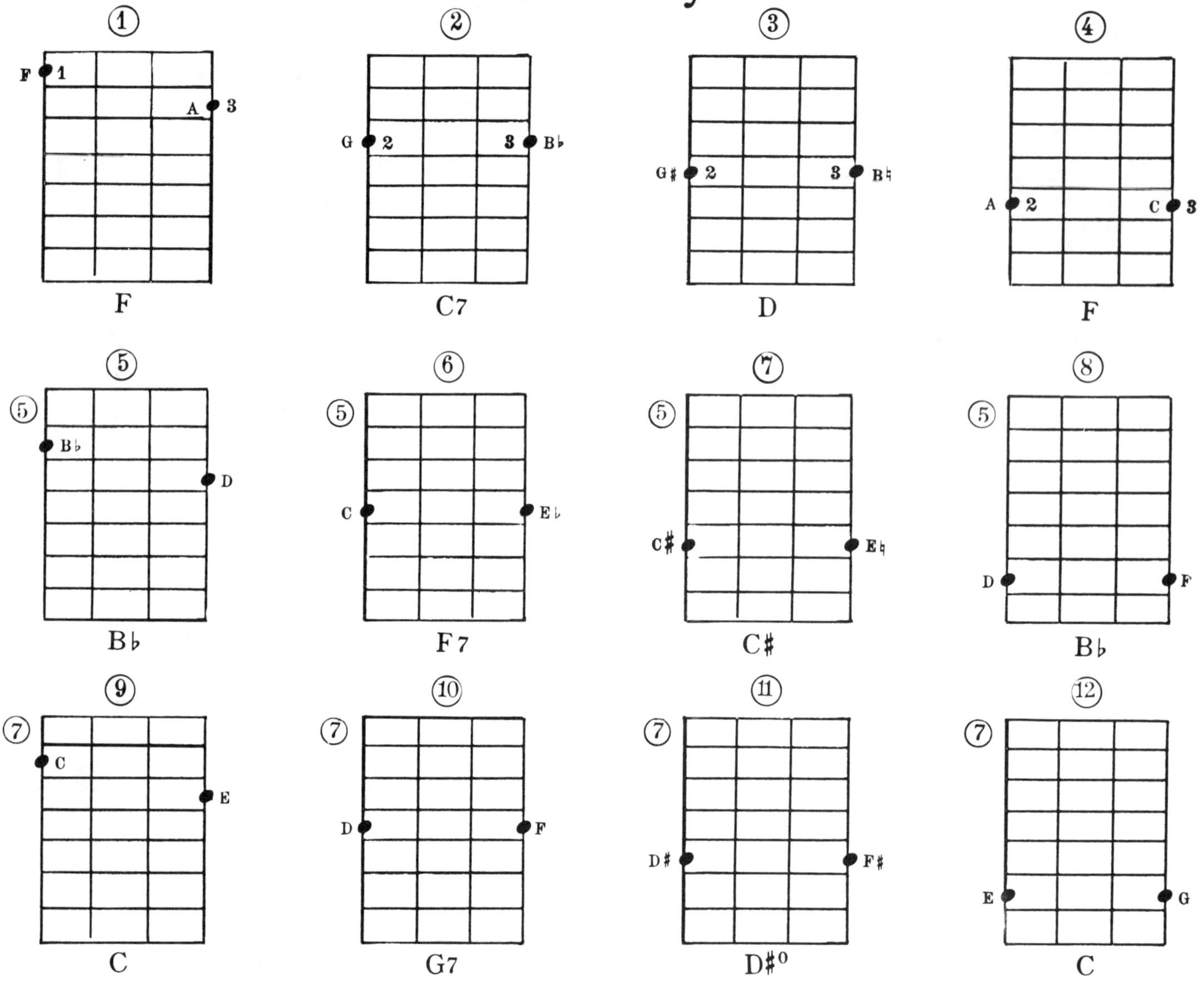

① F 1 · A 3 — F

② G 2 · 3 B♭ — C7

③ G♯ 2 · 3 B♮ — D

④ A 2 · C 3 — F

⑤ ⑤ B♭ · D — B♭

⑥ ⑤ C · E♭ — F 7

⑦ ⑤ C♯ · E♮ — C♯

⑧ ⑤ D · F — B♭

⑨ ⑦ C · E — C

⑩ ⑦ D · F — G7

⑪ ⑦ D♯ · F♯ — D♯°

⑫ ⑦ E · G — C

Tenths Study

On 4th and 1st Strings

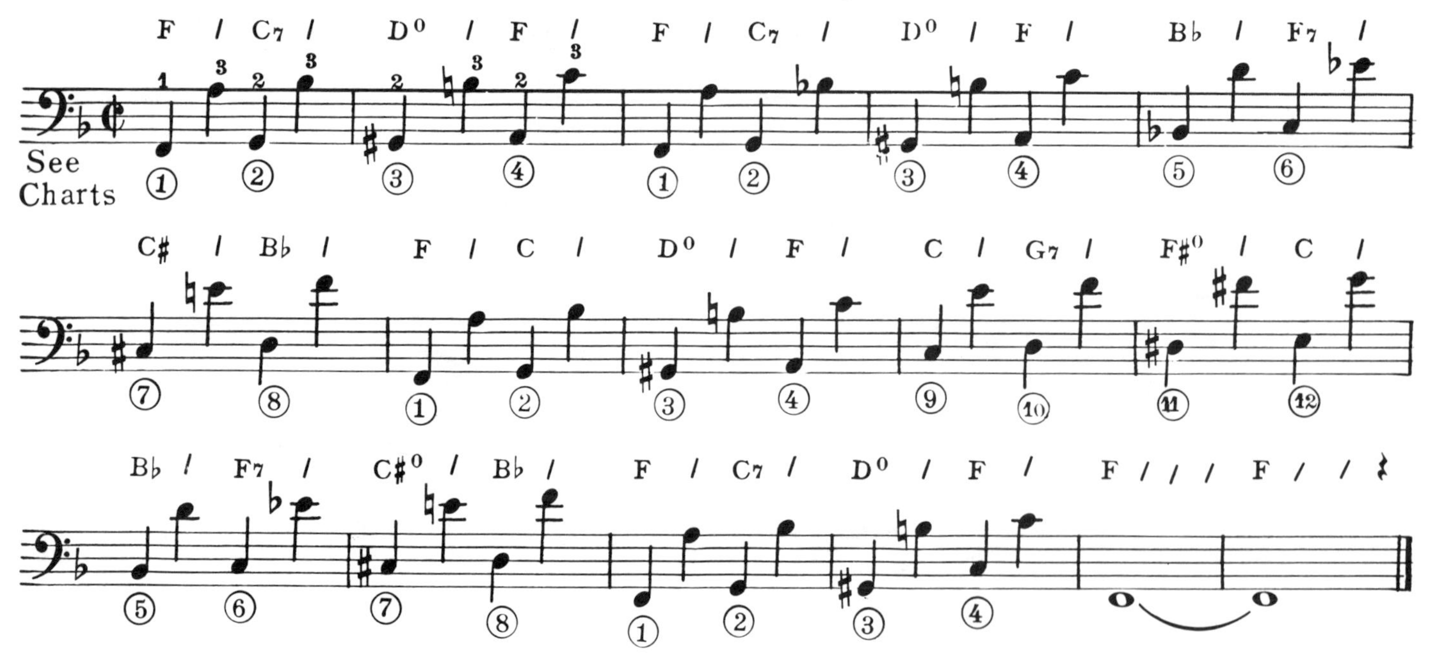

ENCIRCLED NUMBER ⑤ DENOTE CHARTS

Octave Study

Using 1st and 3rd fingers on 4th and 2nd strings.

Little Brown Jug

Practice in First Position—
Then study with Fingering as marked in Fifth Position.

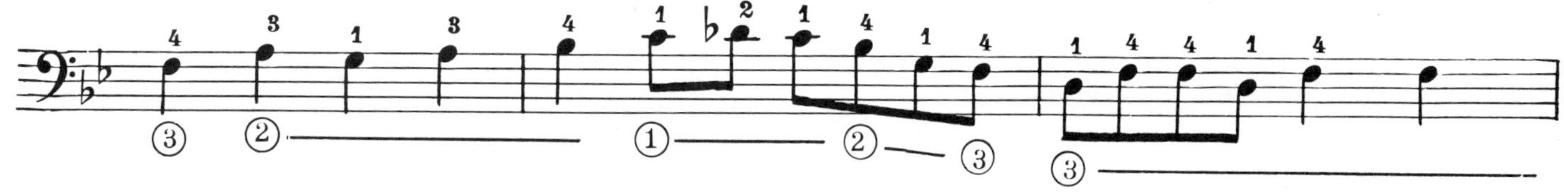

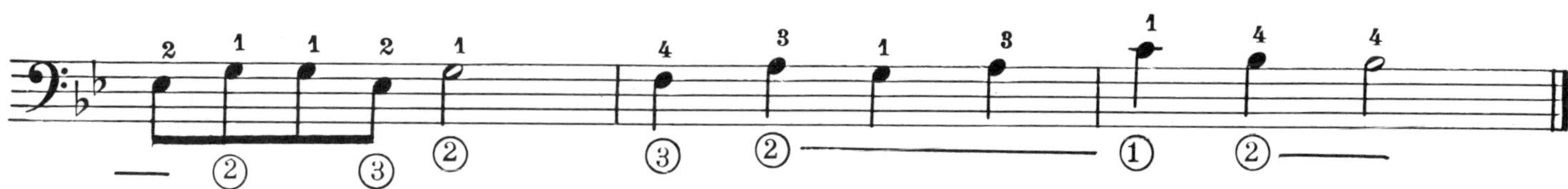

The C MAJOR SCALE in 2nd Position and 7th Position are FINGERED ALIKE

The following Examples should be very interesting as well as informative to the serious student

No. 1
2nd Pos.

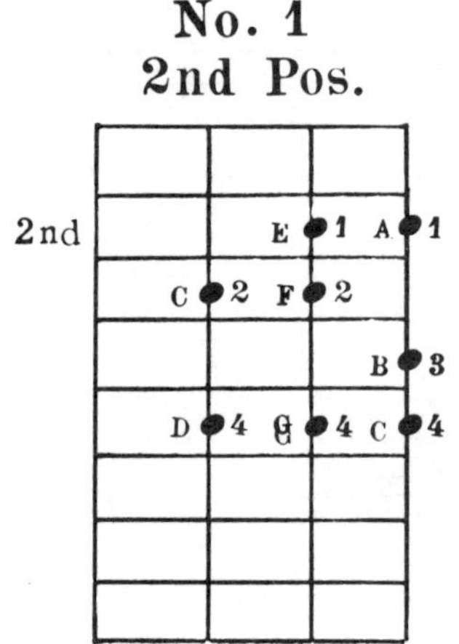

No. 2
7th Pos.

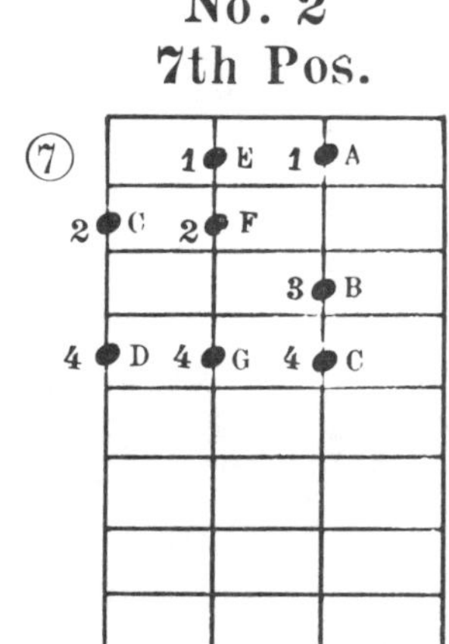

Seventh Position Scale

Containing B♭

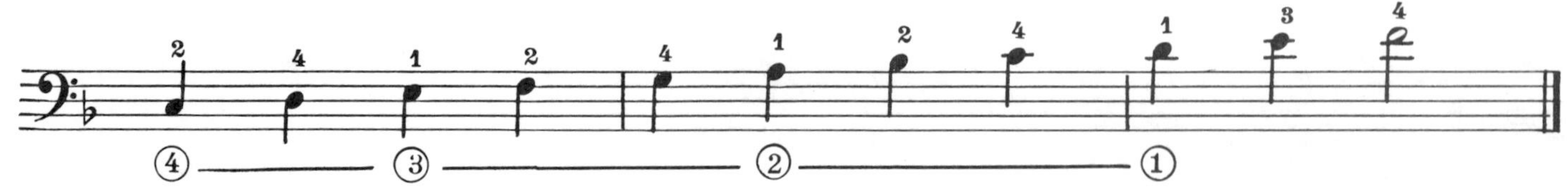

American Patrol

(A Study in Syncopation) 7th position

CHORD CHART

showing the Note-Spelling of the Chords used in modern Electric Bass Parts.

NAME of CHORD	MAJOR	MINOR	AUG.	SEVENTH	DIM.	MINOR SIXTH	MAJOR SIXTH	MINOR SEVENTH	MAJOR SEVENTH	NINTH
C	C E G	C E♭ G	C E G♯	C E G B♭	C E♭ F♯ A	C E♭ G A	C E G A	C E♭ G B♭	C E G B	C E G B♭ D
C♯	C♯ E♯ G♯	C♯ E G♯	C♯ E♯ G×	C♯ E♯ G♯ B	C♯ E G B♭	C♯ E G♯ A♯	C♯ E♯ G♯ A♯	C♯ E G♯ B	C♯ E♯ G♯ B♯	C♯ E♯ G♯ B♮ D♯
D♭	D♭ F A♭	D♭ F♭ A♭	D♭ F A♮	D♭ F A♭ C♭	D♭ E G B♭	D♭ F♭ A♭ B♭	D♭ F A♭ B♭	D♭ F♭ A♭ C♭	D♭ F A♭ C	D♭ F A♭ C♭ E♭
D	D F♯ A	D F A	D F♯ A♯	D F♯ A C	D F A♭ B	D F A B	D F♯ A B	D F A C	D F♯ A C♯	D F♯ A C E
E♭	E♭ G B♭	E♭ G♭ B♭	E♭ G B	E♭ G B♭ D♭	E♭ G♭ A C	E♭ G♭ B♭ C	E♭ G B♭ C	E♭ G♭ B♭ D♭	E♭ G B♭ D	E♭ G B♭ D♭ F
E	E G♯ B	E G B	E G♯ B♯	E G♯ B D	E G B♭ D♭	E G B C♯	E G♯ B C♯	E G B D	E G♯ B D♯	E G♯ B D F♯
F	F A C	F A♭ C	F A C♯	F A C E♭	F A♭ B D	F A♭ C D	F A C D	F A♭ C E♭	F A C E	F A C E♭ G
F♯	F♯ A♯ C♯	F♯ A C♯	F♯ A♯ C×	F♯ A♯ C♯ E	F♯ A C E♭	F♯ A C♯ D♯	F♯ A♯ C♯ D♯	F♯ A C♯ E	F♯ A♯ C♯ E♯	F♯ A♯ C♯ E G♯
G♭	G♭ B♭ D♭	G♭ B♭♭ D♭	G♭ B♭ D	G♭ B♭ D♭ F♭	G♭ A C E♭	G♭ B♭♭ D♭ E♭	G♭ B♭ D♭ E♭	G♭ B♭♭ D♭ F♭	G♭ B♭ D♭ F♮	G♭ B♭ D♭ F♭ A♭
G	G B D	G B♭ D	G B D♯	G B D F	G B♭ D♭ E	G B♭ D E	G B D E	G B♭ D F	G B D F♯	G B D F A
A♭	A♭ C E♭	A♭ C♭ E♭	A♭ C E	A♭ C E♭ G♭	A♭ B D F	A♭ C♭ E♭ F	A♭ C E♭ F	A♭ C♭ E♭ G♭	A♭ C E♭ G	A♭ C E♭ G♭ B♭
A	A C♯ E	A C E	A C♯ E♯	A C♯ E G	A C E♭ G♭	A C E F♯	A C♯ E F♯	A C E G	A C♯ E G♯	A C♯ E G B
B♭	B♭ D F	B♭ D♭ F	B♭ D F♯	B♭ D F A♭	B♭ D♭ E G	B♭ D♭ F G	B♭ D F G	B♭ D♭ F A♭	B♭ D F A	B♭ D F A♭ C
B	B D♯ F♯	B D F♯	B D♯ F×	B D♯ F♯ A	B D F A♭	B D F♯ G♯	B D♯ F♯ G♯	B D F♯ A	B D♯ F♯ A♯	B D♯ F♯ A C♯